Tell Someone

YOU CAN SHARE
THE
GOOD NEWS

GREG LAURIE

LifeWay Press®
Nashville, Tennessee

Published by LifeWay Press® • © 2016 Greg Laurie • Reprinted May 2017

ISBN 978-1-4300-5183-1 • Item 005776124

Dewey decimal classification: 248.5
Subject headings: WITNESSING \ EVANGELISTIC WORK \ GOSPEL

To order additional copies of this resource, write to LifeWay Resources Customer Service; One LifeWay Plaza; Nashville, TN 37234-0113; fax 615-251-5933; phone toll free 800-458-2772; order online at lifeway.com; email orderentry@lifeway.com; or visit the LifeWay Christian Store serving you.

Printed in the United States of America

Groups Ministry Publishing • LifeWay Resources • One LifeWay Plaza • Nashville, TN 37234-0152

Contents

About the Author

GREG LAURIE is the senior pastor of Harvest Christian Fellowship in Riverside and Orange County in California. Harvest is one of the largest churches in the United States and consistently ranks among the most influential churches in the country. He recently celebrated 40 years as the senior pastor. In 1990, he began holding large-scale public evangelistic events called Harvest Crusades. More than 5 million people have attended Harvest events around the world, and more than 5 hundred thousand people have registered professions of faith through these outreaches.

He is the featured speaker of the nationally syndicated radio program "A New Beginning," which is broadcast on more than seven hundred radio outlets worldwide. Along with his work at Harvest Ministries, he served as the 2013 honorary chairman of the National Day of Prayer and also serves on the board of directors of the Billy Graham Evangelistic Association.

He has authored over 70 books, including *As It Is in Heaven, Revelation: The Next Dimension, As I See It, Hope for Hurting Hearts, Married. Happily, Every Day with Jesus, Signs of the Times, Hope for America,* and his autobiography, *Lost Boy.*

He has been married to Cathe Laurie for 41 years, and they have 2 sons, Christopher and Jonathan. Christopher went to be with the Lord in 2008. They also have 5 grandchildren.

Introduction

This is what every follower of Jesus should be engaged in on a regular basis:

SHARING our faith,
LEADING others to Christ,
DISCIPLING them,
and HELPING them to get grounded in the church—
and then GOING out and DOING it all again.

This study is not written to make you feel bad or condemn you if you haven't engaged others with the gospel message.

This study is written to
ENCOURAGE and EQUIP you.

I want to share some stories from my own life of both failure and success in my attempts to share my faith. But the most important things you will find in this study are biblical principles that you can apply in your life. I have put these principles to the test over 40 years of ministry in both one-on-one occasions and large-scale evangelistic events in arenas and stadiums.

If you will take the time to attend these six group sessions, engage in the conversations, and complete the exercises in this book from beginning to end, I believe that as you apply these biblical truths, you will not only be able to share your faith, but also bring others to Christ.

How to Use This Study

This Bible study book includes six weeks of content for group and personal study.

GROUP SESSIONS

Regardless of what day of the week your group meets, each week of content begins with the group session. This group session is designed to be one hour or more—half of the time being teaching and half being personal interaction. Of course it's even better if your group is able to meet longer than an hour, allowing more time for participants to interact with one another.

Each group session uses the following format to facilitate simple yet meaningful interaction among group members, with God's Word, and with the video teaching by Greg Laurie.

START

This page includes questions to get the conversation started, to review the previous week's practical application, and to introduce the video segment.

WATCH

This page includes key points from Greg Laurie's teaching, along with blanks for taking notes as participants watch the video.

RESPOND

This page includes questions and statements that guide the group to respond to Greg Laurie's video teaching and to relevant Bible passages.

PERSONAL STUDY

Each week provides three personal Bible studies with relevant Scripture, learning activities for individual engagement between group sessions, and practical application.

Each week's personal study helps members identify ways they can share the gospel in their daily lives. These personal exercises will build upon one another to encourage and equip participants with everything they need to begin telling their stories in a way that points to the ultimate story: the good news of Jesus Christ.

If only completing one section of the personal study each week, participants will want to fill out the exercises in Personal Study 1. Those exercises focus very specifically on the unique opportunities each person has to share the gospel and what evangelism looks like within each person's circle of influence.

PERSONAL PLAN

At the end of the six weeks, the final pages of this book contain space to gather the key steps from each week in a personal plan for sharing the gospel. Each person can tell someone how his or her life has been changed by the gospel.

ALSO AVAILABLE

This study is based on the book by the same name from Greg Laurie. To get the most out of this experience, everyone can also read:

Tell Someone: How to Share the Good News (B&H, 2016) ISBN 978-1-4336-9014-3.

Books are available for individual or bulk purchase for groups and churches at *lifeway.com/tellsomeone.*

Tips for Leading a Group

PRAYERFULLY PREPARE

Prepare for each meeting by—

REVIEWING the weekly material and group questions ahead of time;

PRAYING for each person in the group.

Ask the Holy Spirit to work through you and the group discussion as you point to Jesus each week through God's Word.

MINIMIZE DISTRACTIONS

Create a comfortable environment. If group members are uncomfortable, they'll be distracted and therefore not engaged in the group experience. Plan ahead by taking into consideration—

SEATING;
TEMPERATURE;
LIGHTING;
FOOD OR DRINK;
SURROUNDING NOISE;
GENERAL CLEANLINESS (put away pets if meeting in a home).

At best, thoughtfulness and hospitality show guests and group members they're welcome and valued in whatever environment you choose to gather. At worst, people may never notice your effort, but they're also not distracted. Do everything in your ability to help people focus on what's most important: connecting with God, with the Bible, and with one another.

ENCOURAGE DISCUSSION

A good small-group experience has the following characteristics.

EVERYONE PARTICIPATES. Encourage everyone to ask questions, share responses, or read aloud.

NO ONE DOMINATES—NOT EVEN THE LEADER. Be sure that your time speaking as a leader takes up less than half of your time together as a group. Politely guide discussion if anyone dominates.

NOBODY IS RUSHED THROUGH QUESTIONS. Don't feel that a moment of silence is a bad thing. People often need time to think about their responses to questions they've just heard or to gain courage to share what God is stirring in their hearts.

INPUT IS AFFIRMED AND FOLLOWED UP. Make sure you point out something true or helpful in a response. Don't just move on. Build community with follow-up questions, asking how other people have experienced similar things or how a truth has shaped their understanding of God and the Scripture you're studying. People are less likely to speak up if they fear that you don't actually want to hear their answers or that you're looking for only a certain answer.

GOD AND HIS WORD ARE CENTRAL. Opinions and experiences can be helpful, but God has given us the Truth. Trust Scripture to be the authority and God's Spirit to work in people's lives. You can't change anyone, but God can. Continually point people to the Word and to active steps of faith.

Tell Someone

INCLUDE OTHERS

Your goal is to foster a community in which people are welcomed just as they are but encouraged to grow spiritually. Always be aware of opportunities to—

INVITE new people to join your group;

INCLUDE any people who visit the group.

An inexpensive way to make first-time guests feel welcome or to invite someone to get involved is to give them their own copies of this Bible study book.

KEEP CONNECTING

Think of ways to connect with group members during the week. Participation during the group session is always improved when members spend time connecting with one another outside the group sessions. The more people are comfortable with and involved in one another's lives, the more they'll look forward to being together. When people move beyond being friendly to truly being friends who form a community, they come to each session eager to engage instead of merely attending.

Encourage group members with thoughts, commitments, or questions from the session by connecting through—

EMAILS;
TEXTS;
SOCIAL MEDIA.

When possible, build deeper friendships by planning or spontaneously inviting group members to join you outside your regularly scheduled group time for—

MEALS;
FUN ACTIVITIES;
PROJECTS AROUND YOUR HOME, CHURCH, OR COMMUNITY.

GROUP INFORMATION

name	contact info

WHY SHARE THE GOSPEL?

Start

Welcome everyone to the first session of *Tell Someone.*

Take a few minutes for participants to introduce themselves if anyone is new to the group. Then start your discussion by asking everyone for a quick answer to the following questions.

What's the most adventurous thing you've ever done? Why did you do it?

When you hear the word *evangelism* **do you think of adventure? If not, what word comes to mind and why?**

For the next six weeks, we'll be studying and discussing personal evangelism. This is something most of us know to be part of the Christian life, but we often feel intimidated by the idea and unsure of what to say.

Greg Laurie has decades of experience as a pastor and evangelist. He's going to share personal experiences, biblical insight, and practical guidance through video teaching in our group and personal study in your books each week.

Here's the spoiler: You can tell someone the good news of Jesus. It's simple. It's also exciting!

Before showing the video for session 1, pray for God to work in your hearts during the next six weeks, beginning right now.

Watch

Use the space below to take notes as you watch session 1.

Did you miss the group session?
Video sessions are available for purchase at *lifeway.com/tellsomeone*

Respond

Respond to the video teaching by discussing the questions below.

As Christians we share the gospel because we're commanded to and because we care. How does this change the way you see evangelism?

READ LUKE 15:7,10,32.

What do the conclusions and the parables of the lost sheep, coin, and son teach us about God? About "lost people?"

Why is leading someone to Christ a joyful celebration?

READ PSALM 126:6.

What does going out weeping have to do with spreading gospel seed and returning with joy?

What did Greg mean by getting mad about people not knowing Jesus?

How does understanding the difference between a sin of commission and omission help you think about the Christian life? About evangelism?

On a scale of 1-10 (1 = dry and stagnate and 10 = full of life) how would you rate your spiritual life? Why? How are giving and receiving both related to spiritual health?

Does anyone have a story to share about a time when you felt spiritually refreshed by sharing your faith, teaching, or discipling someone?

Before closing in prayer, are there any final thoughts from today's video?

We can't control whether or not someone believes the gospel, but we can control whether or not we share it. This week's personal study will help you identify people in your life needing to hear the Good News of Jesus.

PERSONAL STUDY 1

SHARING STARTS WITH CARING

As we get started, I want to tell you how the time between your group sessions will work over the next six weeks. Between each group time of the video teaching and discussion, this book has three "days" or sections of personal reflection and study. These are designed to fit your life no matter where you are or what you prefer.

- If you want to do the three sections on three different days of the week, that's great. Or this may be an every other day pattern for you. Choose a routine that works best for your schedule.
- If you get excited about something, feel free to do as much as you'd like at one time. Of course my hope is that you *will* be excited, but if you are intimidated, unsure, or simply not excited right now, my prayer is that you will jump at the opportunity to tell someone—tell everyone—the good news of Jesus Christ.
- The first section of each session is the most important. If you only do one thing each week, please do Personal Study 1. The very first thing on the pages following the group session is a practical step to consider what all of this looks like in your own life. By the end of the six sessions, you will be able to see how each practical step has mapped out a personal action plan for fulfilling the Great Commission.

The point of this study isn't to hear what I have to say about evangelism, it's to encourage and equip YOU to tell someone.

Today you'll consider the people in your life. We all have more relationships than we realize. Some relationships are closer than others, but we have regular interactions or connections with all kinds of people. They may be friends, family members, coworkers, neighbors, people at the gym, parents of your children's friends, that old classmate you still interact with on social media, etc.

For each category of relationship listed below, write down the names of as many people as you can (whether or not you like the person). Begin with the people of whose salvation you are unsure.

Friends

Family and Relatives

Coworkers and Associates

Neighbors

People you know through activities

People who attend church but may not yet be saved

People with whom you regularly interact on social media

Other

Now go back and circle the names of people with whom you interact most often. Next star the names of people with whom you have the closest relationship. (These may be people you have circled already or people you are close to but don't interact with often.)

Do you see what is happening? You have key connections with people who need a personal relationship with God.

You probably care about some of these people more than others, that's natural. It's OK to want to circle or star their names more obviously, but we need to care about everyone's salvation. Why? God cares.

Sometimes it's easier to talk to people we are closest to. Other times it can be easier to talk to people with whom we have a minimal or passing relationship—like a parent on a team, someone at the gym, a taxi driver.

Do you care that people in your life don't know the Lord? No, really. Consider your thoughts, feelings, and actions, and answer the following questions as honestly as possible.

On a scale of 0-10, how often do you think about the spiritual condition of the people you know (0 = never, 10 = constantly)?

0 1 2 3 4 5 6 7 8 9 10

What would help increase this number, keeping people's spiritual condition in the front of your mind?

On a scale of 0-10, how urgent is it for people to hear and respond to the gospel? (0 = not urgent at all, 10 = extremely urgent)?

0	1	2	3	4	5	6	7	8	9	10

In your own words, describe the difference in someone's eternal reality based on his or her response to the gospel.

In what ways does keeping this eternal reality in mind increase your sense of urgency to share the gospel?

How do you feel about unbelievers?

As I said, some of these people may be more friendly and receptive to the gospel; others may be more defensive or even antagonistic about the Christian faith. We'll talk more about those things later. But far too often we see certain people as the enemy when, in reality, they are bound by the Enemy.

Effective sharing of your faith starts with a CONCERN and a BURDEN.

Over the next six weeks, we'll keeping moving one step at a time toward a confidence and joy in telling people about the good news of Jesus Christ. Every follower of Jesus should be regularly sharing his or her faith, leading others to Christ, discipling them, and helping them get grounded in the church—and then going out and doing it all again.

PERSONAL STUDY 2

SHARING THE GOSPEL IS AN ADVENTURE

Next to personally knowing Jesus Christ as my Savior and Lord, the greatest joy I know is leading others to Christ and watching them grow spiritually. And you can do that, too. It should be a joyful, happy thing to tell others about your relationship with God and explain how they can have one as well.

I have found that the HAPPIEST Christians are the EVANGELISTIC ones.

I have also found that the unhappiest Christians are the nitpicky ones. They are so busy arguing about things inside the church and in the surround culture that they miss opportunities to share the gospel and literally change someone's life forever.

As the old country preacher Vance Havner used to say, "If we are too busy using our sickles on each other, we will miss the harvest!"

We are writing these things
so that our joy may be complete.
1 JOHN 1:4

How would you summarize what John is saying in this verse?

There is a happiness we miss out on if we are not sharing our faith. Don't miss it!

Scripture also tells us that Jesus said:

"It is more blessed to give than to receive."
ACTS 20:35

What does this verse mean?

When have you experienced great joy in giving something to someone?

Why did it bless you as much or more than it blessed the other person?

God doesn't just expect us to give. He has set the ultimate example.

For God loved the world in this way:
He gave His One and Only Son,
so that everyone who believes in Him
will not perish but have eternal life.
JOHN 3:16

God has given His Son. He's given us His Word, the Bible. He's given the Holy Spirit to be with us each day. He's given us an opportunity to not only have eternal life in heaven, but abundant life and joy in the world right now.

Understand, this study is not intended to make you feel bad or condemn you if you have not engaged others with the gospel message. This study was written to encourage, inspire, and revitalize you.

Those who refresh others will themselves be refreshed.
PROVERBS 11:25, NLT

If you've shared the gospel or been blessed to lead someone to Jesus, in what ways did it energize your own faith and enthusiasm?

How did it give that person(s) a new and noticeable change in his life or in her life?

God hasn't blessed you with all the messages you've heard in church or read in books over the years for you to keep it to yourself. Have you seen the TV programs that show the lifestyle of what they call "hoarders"? I'm not talking about people who just keep a few things too long. These are people who've filled their homes, their garages, and every square inch of their space with stuff. It takes days to clear it out.

Sometimes as Christians we can be the same way—hoarding all God has given us and not sharing it with others. Remember this: you are blessed to be a blessing. So let's get the idea out of our heads that sharing our faith is something we can't do or something miserable to engage in. Nothing could be further from the truth.

If you'll take the time to go through this study from beginning to end and apply the biblical truths, I believe you will be able to not only share your faith but to bring others to Christ.

> *Though one goes along weeping,*
> *carrying the bag of seed,*
> *he will surely come back with shouts of joy,*
> *carrying his sheaves.*
> **PSALM 126:6**

Jesus told us there is joy in heaven over every sinner who comes to repentance. (See Luke 15:7.) If heaven gets excited, we should get excited, too!

No doubt about it, new believers are the lifeblood of the church. They also are the lifeblood of the Christian. We all need new believers in our lives. We need to deepen and ground them. In turn, they reignite and excite us.

You show me a church that doesn't have a constant flow of new Christians coming in, and I'll show you a church that's stagnating.

We have a choice: EVANGELIZE or FOSSILIZE!

PERSONAL STUDY 3

WE'RE COMMANDED TO SHARE THE GOSPEL

We share the gospel because we care and because we are commanded to do so.

All authority has been given to Me in heaven and on earth. Go, therefore, and make disciples of all nations, baptizing them in the name of the Father and of the Son and of the Holy Spirit, teaching them to observe everything I have commanded you. And remember, I am with you always, to the end of the age.
MATTHEW 28:18-20

Go into all the world and preach the Good News to everyone.
MARK 16:15, NLT

Why tell others about Jesus Christ? Here's the short answer: Jesus told us to.

In fact, Jesus commanded us to take this message to the ends of the earth. The verses above are commonly known as the Great Commission. Another way to think of this is as a co-mission. This is a mission for every one of us to carry out together.

According to Jesus' words in the verses above, what did Jesus command His followers to do?

To what group of people are followers of Jesus commanded to go?

What's the first word, thought, or feeling that pops into your mind when hearing the words "authority" and "command"?

Do you think of Jesus more in the past tense (He said and did things in the past) or in the present tense (His words still apply and He's at work in and through you today)? Explain your answer.

Does the fact that Jesus has "all authority" and "commanded" His followers to do these things fit with your picture of Jesus? Why or why not?

Jesus' words are a command. It was never a mere suggestion that we, His followers, bring the gospel to others if we feel like it. This was, and is, as they say in the military, a direct order!

So, let's put this together: the Great Commission is to preach and teach; it's to proclaim and disciple.

In the Great Commission, we're commanded by Jesus to go and verbally communicate His good news of salvation to as many people as we can. If they respond to this message, we're to "make disciples" of them. That is, we're to help them become grounded in their faith and integrated into a local church. Then, we're to go and repeat this process.

Paul writes:

> *We proclaim Christ! We warn everyone we meet, and we teach everyone we can, all that we know about him, so that, if possible, we may bring every man up to his full maturity in Christ.*
> **COLOSSIANS 1:28, PHILLIPS**

Tell Someone

That's the objective: lead people to Jesus and bring them to maturity.

God says He is looking for people He can "show Himself strong for" (2 Chron. 16:9).

That is where you come in. God wants to use YOU to bring other people to HIMSELF.

You might protest, "God could never use someone like me!" Actually He can and will if you let Him. It could even happen before the day is over. He won't force you to share your faith, but He will prompt you. And when you take that step of faith, He'll empower and use you.

What's your excuse?

Think of Moses. When called by God to speak out for Him, Moses essentially said, "I can't. I have a speech impediment!" (See Ex. 4:10.) When called by God to speak, Jeremiah felt he was too young. (See Jer. 1:6.) Think of those God used who had challenges and failures in life: Noah got drunk. Abraham was old. Jacob was a liar. David had an affair. Peter denied Christ. The disciples fell asleep while praying. Timothy had an ulcer. Lazarus was dead!

Paul wrote, "We now have this light shining in our hearts, but we ourselves are like fragile clay jars containing this great treasure. This makes it clear that our great power is from God, not from ourselves" (2 Cor. 4:7, NLT).

I want you to discover the adventure of being used by God, especially in the area of telling others about Jesus.

God says He's looking for people He can "show Himself strong for" (2 Chron. 16:9). He's searching for someone who, like the prophet Isaiah, will simply say, "Here I am. Send me" (Isa. 6:8). Would you be that person? If so, a wonderful adventure awaits you.

Remember, God doesn't call the qualified; He qualifies the called.

God isn't looking for ABILITY as much as He's looking for AVAILABILITY.

Write a prayer asking God for a passion and boldness to share the gospel. Ask for conviction that prompts obedience and a joy in obedient steps of faith. Thank Him for inviting you to join His work of seeking and saving the lost so that there will be great celebration in heaven.

WEEK 2

WHEN & WHERE TO SHARE THE GOSPEL

START

Start by welcoming everyone back to the second session of *Tell Someone*. Ask group members the following questions to review the past week's study and to introduce this week's topic.

Last week we looked at the two main reasons we share the gospel.

1. We share because we're commanded to by Jesus.
2. We share because we care about others.

The first day of your personal study helped you identify different people in your life. Who was surprised by the number of people you identified?

Was it more or less people than you would've guessed?

Of those people, to whom do you feel a particular burden for their need for Jesus?

Encourage group members to be praying for one another each week and for the people in their lives needing salvation.

Before showing the video for session 2, pray for God to help people in your group recognize opportunities to share the gospel.

WATCH

Use the space below to take notes as you watch session 2.

Did you miss the group session?
Video sessions are available for purchase at *lifeway.com/tellsomeone*

RESPOND

Respond to the video teaching by discussing the questions below.

On a scale of 1-10 (1 = low and 10 = high) how would you rate your readiness to share the gospel? Your awareness of opportunities? Why?

When and where are you around people needing the gospel?

Apart from Christ, in what ways do you see other people trying to fill the hole in their lives? How have you tried to fill that hole in your life?

READ ROMANS 10:9-15.

Why is it not enough to be a good moral example to non-believers?

Is there someone in your life that you don't want to share with or think that person would never repent and believe? Why?

Greg asked if we'd considered that God may have us where we are for a reason. How does this change your perspective on life? On evangelism?

READ 2 TIMOTHY 4:2.

If God doesn't usually speak audibly, how have you experienced Him providing opportunities to share the gospel?

How can you be more intentional about interacting with people in your daily routines?

What else has been challenging or encouraging from today's session?

This week pay attention to the places you go and time you spend that could provide opportunities to share the gospel. Next week be ready to share what you've observed about opportunities to interact with nonbelievers.

PERSONAL STUDY 1

WHEN AND WHERE CAN YOU SHARE THE GOSPEL?

Last week we focused on why we should share the gospel. This week we're answering when and where we should share the gospel. You don't have to be a Bible scholar to understand the original Greek language of Jesus' words in the Great Commission.

"Go into all the world and preach the gospel."
MARK 16:15

The answer is simple: Right now, wherever you are, and wherever you go. It helps to keep this in mind by personalizing the command.

Go into all of YOUR FAMILY and preach the gospel.

Go into all of YOUR WORKPLACE and preach the gospel.

Go into all of YOUR NEIGHBORHOOD and preach the gospel.

Go into all of YOUR WORLD and preach the gospel.

At the end of Matthew's Gospel, Jesus put it this way.

> *"God authorized and commanded me to commission you: Go out and train everyone you meet, far and near, in this way of life, marking them by baptism in the threefold name: Father, Son, and Holy Spirit. Then instruct them in the practice of all I have commanded you. I'll be with you as you do this, day after day after day, right up to the end of the age."*
> **MATTHEW 28:18-20, MSG**

I love that don't you? There's no mistaking what Jesus is saying. It's a command.

"Go out and train everyone you meet, far and near."

Just like you have more relationships than you may have realized, you may go more places than you usually think about.

Think through your regular schedule each week using the calendar on the following pages.

1. **In each daily column, list places you go in a typical week.**
2. **In the "Less Frequently" sections, identify places you go within your community less often such as a library, park, shopping areas, usual business trips, etc.**
3. **Using the "Special Occasions" sections, identify places you go on rare occasions such as vacation, holidays, visiting family, occasional business trips, etc.**
4. **Estimate the amount of time spent each day outside of your home by adding up time spent just in your typical week. Write that time in the "Total Time" column.**

God has put more people in your lives in more places than you likely ever realized. This is no coincidence. We'll look at that in the following sections of this week's study.

Tell Someone

Where do I go and when?

Sunday	Monday	Tuesday	Wednesday

Less Frequently

Special Occasions

Thursday	Friday	Saturday	Total Time

Less Frequently

Special Occasions

PERSONAL STUDY 2

WHEN SHOULD YOU SHARE THE GOSPEL?

One of my favorite stories in the Old Testament is of the strikingly beautiful Jewish girl named Hadassah. She won a nationwide beauty contest staged by the king of Persia. Her prize was becoming the next queen of the kingdom. From that point on, she became known as Queen Esther.

If you have time, I encourage you to grab your Bible and read the whole story. You can find it in the Old Testament book appropriately titled Esther. It's a short but wonderful story filled with humor, suspense, and surprises.

The Book of Esther reads like a fairy tale, including a very dark plot twist. But this story is real. It's history. A villain even more sinister than any child's story would produce emerges with a plan to exterminate the Jewish people. His name was Haman. But Queen Esther was disconnected from the needs of her people, as she lived a life of pampered luxury in the safety and comfort of the royal palace.

So, her uncle Mordecai covered himself in sackcloth and stood outside the palace. Alerted to this, the queen sent him a change of clothes. Talk about missing the point! She was oblivious to the plight of her people until her uncle sent her this message:

> *If you keep quiet at a time like this, deliverance and relief for the Jews will arise from some other place, but you and your relatives will die. Who knows if perhaps you were made queen for just such a time as this?*
>
> **ESTHER 4:14, NLT**

Allow me to loosely paraphrase this statement: "Esther, you're not where you are by coincidence, but by providence. You're in a position to potentially save people. If you don't do it, God will find someone else. But did it ever occur to you that you're where you are for this very moment?"

Describe how it makes you feel to know that God has a plan for your life?

How does it change the way you see the world around you knowing that God is at work?

We can be just like Queen Esther, happily ensconced in the security of the church and surrounded by our Christian friends as we watch Christian movies, listen to Christian radio, read Christian books, and spend our money with Christian businesses. (These are all good things, by the way!) We can easily find ourselves living in a Christian bubble and having little to no contact with the world around us filled with lost people. When that happens, we're missing amazing opportunities to be used by God.

> Jesus didn't say that the whole world should GO TO CHURCH, but He did say that the church should GO TO THE WHOLE WORLD.

God wants you to go into all of your world and preach the gospel! Esther was placed where she was "for such a time as this," and so are you.

Think back to the activity in the previous section. Where do you go that you look forward to each week or during the year?

Why do you look forward to this place?

Tell Someone

Where do you go that you dread? In other words, if you could remove it from your calendar, you'd do so in an instant. Why do you dislike this place?

Is there someplace that feels absolutely hopeless, like there's no way God is at work? Where is it, and why do you feel that way?

Think back to the people you don't enjoy being around. (Don't write their names down!) Why does that person(s) pop into your mind?

Did it ever occur to you that you are right where God wants you to be? That irritating neighbor, the disagreeable coworker, the spiteful or dramatic family member are part of your life so you can reach them with the message of the gospel!

Start by praying for them. It's hard to continue to think of a person as an enemy when you pray for him or her. Instead of trying to wiggle out of where you are, why not look for "divine appointments"? You are where you are for "such a time as this."

The primary way God has chosen to reach people is through other people. And the primary way He works through people is through the verbalization of the gospel. This has always been true. Paul wrote in his letter to the Christians in Rome:

How can they hear about him unless someone tells them?
ROMANS 10:14, NLT

Ultimately, Jesus is the one who has saved us. He is King of kings and Lord of lords. Christ has defeated our great Enemy. Yet He has also given us an urgent message in His perfect timing.

Remember, lives are at stake. You and I are positioned strategically in order to see people saved from death and given eternal life. What are you waiting for? Step out. Take a risk. It's worth it. You have the good news that will change everything.

The gospel is ONLY GOOD NEWS
if it gets there ON TIME.

PERSONAL STUDY 3

WHERE SHOULD YOU SHARE THE GOSPEL?

There's another amazing story in the Bible about a man named Jonah. It's also found in the Old Testament, and I encourage you to look it up and read the whole thing. You may have guessed that his story can be found in … the Book of Jonah. His story is even shorter than Esther's, but every bit as exciting.

You've probably heard the story of Jonah being swallowed by a big fish and spit out 3 days later. I like to call him the regurgitated prophet. We see both sins of commission and omission in Jonah's story.

- Jonah had sins of **commission**—he literally ran in the opposite direction of the mission God had given him. He acted contrary to what God had said.
- Jonah also had sins of **omission**—he wasn't speaking up when, where, and to whom God had commanded him to preach. This prophet wasn't sharing God's message with other people.

This wasn't a matter of Jonah mustering up the courage to speak to a person or two. This is like a foreshadowing of the Great Commission in that Jonah was commanded to take God's message to a people group outside of Jewish heritage. He was literally told to proclaim God's judgment of sin to a foreign culture. If that wasn't enough, the foreign people group was a brutal enemy of the Jewish people to whom Jonah belonged.

Where are you around people who need to hear the gospel?

On the shores of Nineveh, Jonah began to preach the message the Lord gave him. I'm not quite sure why Jonah ran from God in the first place. Perhaps he was afraid of rejection. You could say he was the original "chicken of the sea." I think perhaps what he really feared was success. In other words, he was afraid God would spare them, and that is exactly what the Lord did.

But instead of rejoicing at their repentance, Jonah was angry. The Bible tells us, "So he complained to the LORD about it: 'Didn't I say before I left home that you would do this, LORD? That is why I ran away to Tarshish! I knew that you are a merciful and compassionate God, slow to get angry and filled with unfailing love. You are eager to turn back from destroying people' " (Jonah 4:2, NLT).

So much for the idea of the "wrathful God" of the Old Testament as compared to the "loving God" of the New Testament. There's only one true God in the Bible, and He is holy, righteous, and perfect. He's also loving, forgiving, and ready to pardon. That's because God loves and cares for lost people, and so should we.

It could be that the reason we don't want to share our faith is the deep-seated fear that the people we speak with will indeed respond and make a commitment to follow Christ. Why? Because we know it's our responsibly to then take them under our wing and help integrate them into our church—and in all honesty, that could be quite the inconvenience.

In what way might helping someone come to faith in Jesus feel like a personal responsibility or inconvenience?

Is there a time and place where you think you can't go out of your way to help someone know Jesus? If so, when and where is it? Why would you not want to go out of your usual routine?

Tell Someone

What would help you keep an attitude of obedience and willingness to share the gospel no matter how intimidating or seemingly inconvenient?

Some Christians don't necessarily want a new Christian hanging around them because some choices in their lives might be potential stumbling blocks to the new believer, and, frankly, they don't want that kind of pressure. But that is exactly one of the reasons we should have a new believer around!

How might your life be a stumbling block?

In what ways can you be a stepping stone to help someone else move closer to Jesus?

When and where are you around someone you could be a stepping stone for in his or her spiritual journey?

Are you a BRIDGE or a BARRIER to people coming to know Jesus Christ?

You are either one or the other. Jonah was called to go and preach to the people of Nineveh, and we have been called to go to our world as well.

Some will set up a false dichotomy and say something along the lines of, "I don't really feel comfortable preaching. I will just be a good example and win people to Christ through the way I live." But Jesus didn't say to merely, "Go into all the world and be a good example." He said, "Go into all the world and preach the gospel."

Write a prayer asking God for boldness to speak up with the message of salvation. If necessary, confess any unwillingness, fear, or other barriers that have kept you from sharing the gospel.

WEEK 3

THE POWER OF YOUR PERSONAL STORY

START

Start by welcoming everyone back to the third session of *Tell Someone.*

Ask group members the following questions to review the past week's study and to introduce this week's topic.

Last week you began to identify when and where you can share the gospel. Who was surprised by the number of places you go or amount of time you spend away from home?

Was it more or less people than you would've guessed?

Of those places, which seem to be the most likely setting for sharing the gospel?

Have you had any opportunities to share the gospel with someone you identified the first week or in any of the places you went last week?

Encourage group members to be praying for one another each week and for the people in their lives needing salvation.

Pray for your time together now and then show the video for session 3.

WATCH

Use the space below to take notes as you watch session 3.

Did you miss the group session?
Video sessions are available for purchase at *lifeway.com/tellsomeone*

RESPOND

Respond to the video teaching by discussing the questions below.

We all love stories. What is your favorite story of all time (book, movie, show, play)? Why?

How does our love for stories relate to sharing the good news of Jesus?

READ JOHN 4:39-42.

How was this woman's story a bridge to Jesus? What does this reveal about the power of someone's personal story of meeting Jesus?

Greg gave four tips for sharing your testimony. With which of the following are you most likely to have trouble? Why?

1. Don't glorify or exaggerate your past.
2. Don't boast about what you gave up for God, but about what he gave up for you.
3. Speak in a language people can understand.
4. Be fool enough to grab it.

Telling your story is powerful bridge for the gospel message. What in your life can be a unique connecting point to another person with similar experiences? How can that part of your story point to the gospel?

How did you come to know Jesus and how has he changed your life?

What else has been challenging or encouraging from today's session?

The assignment for this week is to think through your personal story and look for opportunities to share it with others. Next week we'll take a few minutes for each of us to share our stories with one another.

PERSONAL STUDY 1

YOU HAVE A STORY TO SHARE

This week we've moved from why, when, and where we should share the gospel to how we go about sharing the gospel. This is where most Christians begin to get nervous. Many believers agree with the principle that they should share the gospel. They just don't know how to practice it.

Once again, I assure you that you already know more than you think. We often overcomplicate evangelism—even the name can sound intimidating. But it's not a rigid formula, sales pitch, or mechanical process where every nut and bolt has to be in the right place to work properly.

One of the best ways to share your faith is to engage a person through story. This week we'll focus on telling your story. Next week we'll look at knowing other people's stories.

The questions in this section will help you discover how your personal story is one of the most effective tools in your evangelistic toolbox. It is often called your "testimony." Everyone who has put his or her faith in Jesus Christ has a testimony. Some are more dramatic than others, but every story is valid, including yours. Don't believe the lie that your story doesn't matter or isn't appropriate to talk about now that you're a Christian. I guarantee someone needs to hear it.

Someone has a STORY a lot like yours but doesn't know there can be a HAPPY ENDING.

Write Your Own Story

Where did you grow up? What was life like in that place?

What were significant moments (high and low) in your life?

What character traits or behaviors (good or bad) resulted from or were revealed in these significant moments?

What was your life like before coming to faith?

What was most important to you?

Where were you seeking satisfaction/joy/purpose?

Tell Someone

How did those pursuits make you feel?

When did you first encounter the gospel?

Who told you? Describe your relationship with that person(s).

What did they say/do?

When did you realize the truth of what they were saying?

What has been your experience after coming to faith in Jesus?
Best part? Hardest part?

Did you have any religious background culturally/personally?

What was your first experience with the church?

What is your favorite thing about the church you are a member of?

What is your favorite part of being in a Bible study group?

What you've just walked through is intended to get you thinking and to help you realize that a lot of these details are points of connection to other people's stories. This isn't a checklist to make sure you have a "good testimony."

There are plenty of other details that are great connection points. Even seemingly "non-spiritual" things like personal interests and hobbies can lead to sharing the gospel with a friend who has your interest for baking or fishing or photography.

The word *testimony* may feel intimidating, but it's simply a matter of you telling someone about your life and how Jesus has changed your story forever.

PERSONAL STUDY 2

BUILD BRIDGES, DON'T BURN THEM

Let's begin by pointing out our objective. Our goal is to build a bridge to our listener, not burn one. I've seen Christians armed with memorized Bible verses and clever arguments completely overwhelm a person in a "gospel barrage."

They may have WON THE DEBATE, but sadly they didn't WIN THE SOUL.

Jesus built bridges. The perfect picture of how He reached out relationally instead of being sidetracked by winning a religious debate can be found in John 4. In this story, Jesus is speaking to a person whom nobody would consider worthy of His attention. She was what we would call "a woman with a reputation." The woman at the well, married and divorced five times, was a Samaritan. Her life story made her a least likely candidate for Jesus to reach out to with the gospel.

Look up John 4:1-45 and read the story of the woman at the well.

What did Jesus do to build a bridge to this woman?

How did she first respond?

This woman was very aware of the bad news in her story and had thought that her story was a tragedy with no happy ending.

In what way is Jesus' interaction with this woman encouraging to you?

In what way is Jesus' interaction with this woman discouraging?

Jesus acknowledged the bad news without condemnation. He didn't shy away from the reality of sin, yet He didn't belittle or shame the woman over her guilt.

Once she recognized and believed the good news, what did she do?

After her conversation with Jesus, she believed in Him and immediately went out and began to tell others. I'm sure everyone knew her story, and they could see the radical transformation that had taken place in her life after her encounter with Jesus Christ.

This woman didn't have any training, formula, or perfect theology. Yet she couldn't wait to tell someone—everyone in earshot—the good news. And look at how people responded to her simple testimony.

> *Many Samaritans from that town believed in Him because of what the woman said when she testified, "He told me everything I ever did." Therefore, when the Samaritans came to Him, they asked Him to stay with them, and He stayed there two days. Many more believed because of what He said. And they told the woman, "We no longer believe because of what you said, for we have heard for ourselves and know that this really is the Savior of the world."*
>
> **JOHN 4:39-42**

Tell Someone

I love the honest enthusiasm of her response, don't you? She couldn't wait to tell others her story about Jesus. She felt free. She was excited. She was telling everyone! Jesus reached out to her and she reached out to others.

As much as I love the story of this woman and her response, I love the response of the people who came to see what she was talking about.

> *"We no longer believe because of what you said, for we have heard for ourselves and know that this really is the Savior of the world."*
> **JOHN 4:42**

This is the goal. Jesus built a bridge to this woman. This woman heard and believed. Then she built a bridge for her entire town to meet Jesus. Her personal story was powerful.

> They were interested in Jesus because of her STORY.
> They believed in Jesus because of their EXPERIENCE.

People can argue all day with you about certain facts. But they can't argue with your personal story of how you came to faith. Using your testimony as a bridge is very effective because it helps find common ground with the people you speak with. They may be surprised that you were not always the way you are now as a Christian—that you didn't always believe what you now believe.

You could say something like, "This is the way I used to think and the way I used to view Christians and the church, but then ..." Fact is, the way you used to think may be the way the person you are speaking with is presently thinking. You're showing him or her how and why you changed your direction in life—how and why you became a follower of Jesus Christ. Perhaps you struggled with drugs and alcohol. Perhaps you were in a life of crime. You may have been living in immorality. Then again, perhaps you weren't addicted to anything and instead were very successful but still had an emptiness in your life.

How do you personally relate to the story of the woman at the well?

What does her story teach us about Jesus?

Let me tell you your story without even knowing you:

- You were in rebellion against God because of your sin.
- You heard the gospel.
- You believed in Jesus and turned from your sin.
- He forgave you of all your sins and gave you a peace and purpose in life.
- Now instead of hell, you're going to heaven.

The main thing is just telling your story. Someone needs to hear it. Every testimony has bad news and good news. The turning point in your life is all about Jesus.

Write a prayer of thanks that Jesus has offered you grace even though He knows your past, your secrets, and your shame.

PERSONAL STUDY 3

PAUL'S EXAMPLE OF BRIDGE BUILDING

It's worth noting that the apostle Paul often used his personal testimony when he spoke. Though he was a brilliant orator and extremely knowledgeable about Scripture, he often started by telling his own story to build a bridge to his listeners. His message before the Roman leader Agrippa is the perfect example.

After talking about the fact that he had been raised in a strict religious Jewish home and that he felt he was doing God's work when he began to hunt down and arrest Christians, he described what happened to change him.

"One day I was on such a mission to Damascus, armed with the authority and commission of the leading priests. About noon, Your Majesty, as I was on the road, a light from heaven brighter than the sun shone down on me and my companions. We all fell down, and I heard a voice saying to me in Aramaic, 'Saul, Saul, why are you persecuting me? It is useless for you to fight against my will.'

'Who are you, Lord?' I asked.

And the Lord replied, 'I am Jesus, the one you are persecuting. Now get to your feet! For I have appeared to you to appoint you as my servant and witness. Tell people that you have seen me, and tell them what I will show you in the future. And I will rescue you from both your own people and the Gentiles.' "

ACTS 26:12-17, NLT

How does Paul's story reveal the fact that Jesus identifies personally with His people?

What encouragement does that provide to you?

If you were with someone of great importance like Paul was, why would your personal story be worth telling?

Certainly Paul had a dramatic testimony. But we can all relate to the fact that Jesus changed our lives. After connecting with Agrippa on a personal level, Paul gets to what it really means to be a Christian.

> *" 'Yes, I am sending you to the Gentiles to open their eyes, so they may turn from darkness to light and from the power of Satan to God. Then they will receive forgiveness for their sins and be given a place among God's people, who are set apart by faith in me.' "*
> **ACTS 26:17-18, NLT**

Underline the phrases in Acts 26:12-18 where Paul clearly states that as a Christian, Jesus expected him to tell others to share the gospel.

After sharing his own story, Paul share a simple gospel, circle the key points in his short gospel summary in Acts 26:17-18.

This is a perfect template to follow. Tell your story then transition to a simple gospel. Following are a few tips about telling your story the right way.

1. Don't glorify or exaggerate your past.

Accuracy is really important. So is truthfulness. Some testimonies get more dramatic with the passing of time. Perhaps people think that makes the story more appealing, but if it's not truthful, that is counterproductive. Just tell the truth about your life and what God did for you. Do you think God needs your made-up story to reach people? Just tell the truth about your past and your present.

Another problem is making your past sound more appealing than your present. I have heard some Christians, in the name of "giving their testimony," go on and on about all the wild parties and fun they had before their conversion. And when they get to the part when they became a believer, it sounds as though their lives ended. If that is the way you are telling the story of how you came to Christ, you are missing all God has done for you.

What one word or phrase would summarize your past?

2. Don't boast about what you gave up for Him, but what He gave up for you.

I've heard people talk about the "great sacrifices" they made to follow Jesus. Compared to what Jesus gave up for you, it's nothing! Paul summed up his past and had everything in perfect perspective when he said,

> *Yes, all the things I once thought were so important are gone from my life. Compared to the high privilege of knowing Christ Jesus as my Master, firsthand, everything I once thought I had going for me is insignificant—dog dung. I've dumped it all in the trash so that I could embrace Christ and be embraced by him.*
> **PHILIPPIANS 3:8, MSG**

Now that's perspective. Fact is, Paul had a very impressive pedigree in his family line and trained under the finest teachers of Israel. But he understood it all meant nothing apart from Christ—"dog dung," thrown in the trash!

Do you think you made a great sacrifice to follow Jesus Christ? Think about it for a moment. You gave up an ever-present guilt, a deep emptiness in your life, and a future separated from God, in hell. Instead, Jesus removed your guilt, filled that void inside, and gave you the certainty of a home in heaven! You gave up nothing in comparison to what Christ gave up to save your soul. Make sure you emphasize that when you share your personal story.

How would you summarize Jesus' sacrifice?

How would you personalize how this changed your view and values?

3. When you tell your story, it's not about you; it's about Him!

Our story is the bridge, not the destination. The point of sharing your story is so you can tell His story: His love for humanity, His death on the cross, and His resurrection from the dead. Just give the big picture and sum it up as Paul did when standing before a Roman leader. He said that he'd turned "from darkness to light" and "from the power of Satan to God," (Acts 26:18, NLT) and now he had an eternal reward and inheritance.

We don't want people marveling over our story, but over His—the sacrifice Jesus made, the price He paid because of His great love for us. When the woman at the well told her story, she pointed to Jesus, and as a result, "many Samaritans from that town believed in Him" (John 4:39). As you tell your story, I pray something similar will happen.

We'll look more at the essential components of the gospel and how to build different bridges from your story to His in upcoming sessions.

HOW TO SHARE THE GOSPEL

START

Start by welcoming everyone back to the fourth session of *Tell Someone*. Ask group members the following questions to review the past week's study and to introduce this week's topic.

Last week you looked at the power of your personal story. What was helpful or encouraging as you thought through your testimony?

Can everyone share a one-minute version of how you came to faith in Jesus and the main way He has changed your life? (Encourage each person to do this as a way to get comfortable talking about their story.)

Did anyone have an opportunity to share your testimony or have conversations about Jesus this past week? If so, what happened?

We've looked at why, when, and where to share the gospel. Last week's focus on your personal story was the first step in *how* to share the gospel. Today we'll look further at how to share the gospel conversationally.

Pray for your time together now and then show the video for session 4.

WATCH

Use the space below to take notes as you watch session 4.

Did you miss the group session?
Video sessions are available for purchase at *lifeway.com/tellsomeone*

RESPOND

Respond to the video teaching by discussing the questions below.

We've now looked at why, when, where, and how to share the gospel.

Is the idea of sharing your faith as a dialogue instead of a monologue encouraging or intimidating? Why?

Why is listening to people important?

READ JOHN 4:1-30.

What does this reveal about Jesus? About how to engage people?

How do we avoid or isolate ourselves from culture? Why do we do this?

What questions have you heard to sidetrack conversations into debates? How do you respond?

What are some questions you can ask a person about themselves to get to know them and what they value in order to share the gospel?

Greg mentioned "chumming" while fishing. What statements can you use to test the waters and to see if a person is spiritually interested?

READ 1 PETER 3:15.

How do you prepare – to be ready? How often do you study your bible? What have been helpful routines or ways of studying your Bible?

What else has been challenging or encouraging from today's session?

The assignment for this week is to seek opportunities to engage someone in a conversation about Jesus. Next week we'll look specifically at the key parts of the gospel.

PERSONAL STUDY 1

JESUS-STYLE EVANGELISM

The first thing I want to do is congratulate and thank you if you've ever even attempted to share your faith in Jesus. You're taking steps toward fulfilling the Great Commission.

Secondly, I want to encourage you if you've never shared the gospel—or you feel like you failed in sharing the gospel. Talking to someone about Jesus and what you believe to be true about a relationship with Him is a wonderful adventure that never looks the same twice. In the video teaching, I've already shared with you my so-called failure and fear when first beginning to tell people about Jesus and how He can change lives.

Any attempt to share the gospel is a successful attempt. A gospel seed has been planted. We don't always get to be the ones harvesting the field, but we can always be ones who spread and water seeds planted in a person's heart.

Even Paul wrote a letter to a church in Corinth where people were arguing about whether Paul or a man name Apollos was a more important leader or more instrumental in salvation and spiritual growth. Look at what he said:

> *I planted the seed in your hearts, and Apollos watered it, but it was God who made it grow. It's not important who does the planting, or who does the watering. What's important is that God makes the seed grow. The one who plants and the one who waters work together with the same purpose. And both will be rewarded for their own hard work. For we are both God's workers. And you are God's field. You are God's building.*
>
> **1 CORINTHIANS 3:6-9, NLT**

Describe how Paul's words make you feel.

The Bible isn't giving you an excuse to feel like you're not a person God uses to share the good news. You've been given the same Great Commission that Jesus commanded the apostles.

Jesus was very clear with His disciples that we won't always see the same results. We all need to spread the gospel seed. But we're not responsible for the results. God brings growth.

Jesus used a parable where seed was thrown onto different types of soil. It was all the same seed, but the results were very different for each area of the ground. He explains the different dynamics at play when it comes to a person's openness to receiving the gospel and what happens afterwards.

The farmer plants seed by taking God's word to others. The seed that fell on the footpath represents those who hear the message, only to have Satan come at once and take it away. The seed on the rocky soil represents those who hear the message and immediately receive it with joy. But since they don't have deep roots, they don't last long. They fall away as soon as they have problems or are persecuted for believing God's word. The seed that fell among the thorns represents others who hear God's word, but all too quickly the message is crowded out by the worries of this life, the lure of wealth, and the desire for other things, so no fruit is produced. And the seed that fell on good soil represents those who hear and accept God's word and produce a harvest of thirty, sixty, or even a hundred times as much as had been planted!

MARK 4:14-20

What different things does Jesus say affect a person's openness to receive the gospel?

What things affect a person's growth after hearing the gospel?

Tell Someone

Let's make this more personal.

Describe a successful or positive experience you've had sharing the gospel with someone. What made this a good experience?

Describe a negative experience when talking about Jesus. What made this feel like a bad experience or even a failure?

Everybody is different. The gospel is going to be received (or not) differently at different times by different people. You're also different. Just like Paul and Apollos were used at different times in different ways, you'll also be used differently by God than other people. This isn't bad—it's just different. While we may be different and the circumstances may be different, the seed of God's Word is the same.

Now put some more pieces together from previous weeks.

How has your personal story helped you engage people with the gospel in places or ways that other people may not have been used by God?

Follow Jesus example. He spoke in different ways and emphasized different things with different people. Even though His entry point for a conversation was different, the overall message was the same.

The gospel is an UNCHANGING MESSAGE for a constantly CHANGING WORLD.

Keep in mind though that the Bible also says what feels like change isn't catching God by surprise.

There is nothing new under the sun.
ECCLESIASTES 1:9

There is no argument or question that hasn't been settled and answered by the gospel. But our aim is discussion that leads to a decision. Remember, the goal is not winning the debate, but winning the soul.

If people can be argued INTO believing the gospel, they can be argued OUT OF believing the gospel.

Write a prayer asking God for the ability to recognize people's needs and how the gospel fills those need. Pray specifically for the different people in your life and how to best engage them lovingly but confidently with the good news of Jesus.

PERSONAL STUDY 2

FISHERS OF MEN (& WOMEN)

Let's continue with the "how" question—how do we begin reaching out to people with the gospel? As I have already stated, our goal is to build a bridge to our listener, not burn one.

Just as you have a story to share—your story building a bridge to God's story—everyone else has a story, too. So, next to knowing how to tell your own story, you need to know your audience, so to speak.

In fact, the more you know about the person you are speaking with, the better. Know this: everyone's favorite subject is themselves. After all, what is the most popular kind of photo today? Selfies, of course.

Ask people questions about their life, their views, their outlook. What do they think about this or that? Don't interrupt. Instead, try to understand what they are saying. Then, lovingly begin to build your bridge.

What questions could you ask someone to know more about possible connection points such as values, past experiences, or needs?

Three years before His final words in the Great Commission, Jesus had been clear in His invitation from the very beginning. Being a disciple of Jesus meant more than learning from His teaching—it meant joining His mission.

Jesus called out to them, "Come, follow me, and I will show you how to fish for people!"
MATTHEW 4:19, NLT

Think back to the woman at the well from our study of John 4. The disciples didn't understand why Jesus would talk to this woman. Clearly He was "fishing." After Jesus engaged her with a simple conversation about being thirsty and needing a drink, He said:

"If you only knew the gift God has for you and who you are speaking to, you would ask me, and I would give you living water."
JOHN 4:10, NLT

This is a great way to engage people. Make a spiritual point and see if they respond. Throw out some truth and see if they bite. It's not a trick but a testing of the waters, really—to see if they are curious or receptive.

Perhaps mention that God answered a prayer for you, blessed you, or is your hope in the middle of chaotic times.

What are some examples of simple statements or questions that can test the waters and peak interest for a spiritual conversation?

Sometimes people will ignore you. Other times they may respond, "What do you mean by that?" The Samaritan woman was intrigued by Jesus' statement, but she also was cynical. Her response may be understood to have a note of sarcasm as she asks who He thinks He is to offer her something greater than "our father Jacob" (John 4:12) who represented the religious tradition and cultural identity of both the Jewish and Samaritan people.

Imagine how Jesus could have answered her. Was He "greater" than Jacob? He created Jacob, and everyone else for that matter! But that certainly would have been too much too soon for this girl. Instead, He continues to appeal to her curiosity. Jesus replied:

"Anyone who drinks this water will soon become thirsty again. But those who drink the water I give will never be thirsty again. It becomes a fresh, bubbling spring within them, giving them eternal life."
JOHN 4:13-14, NLT

Jesus was using the water this woman drew from the well as a metaphor for life in general. People draw from various "wells" that can never satisfy their deepest needs and desires—material possessions, success, pleasure, etc.

From what "wells" do most people around you seek satisfaction or relief?

What wells did you draw from before encountering Living Water?

Jesus continued to engage her, reeling her in a little closer with each exchange until He finally gets to the point—He knows her past and offers a new life of grace and freedom. If you remember, she is so overjoyed and in awe of Jesus that she tells everyone her story. She immediately throws out not just a line but a broad net to draw people to Christ!

However, we know this is not always the case. Most conversations won't result in immediate and enthusiastic belief. And certainly we know that every conversation doesn't lead to citywide revival!

Even Jesus had different CONVERSATIONS with different PEOPLE with different OUTCOMES.

Look at the story immediately before this one in John 3. The two people are polar opposites, and so are the immediate outcomes. One was a woman; the other was a man. She was looked down upon; he was looked up to. She was a social outsider; he was a religious leader. Jesus was waiting for the woman in the middle of the day; the man came to Jesus in the middle of the night. But look at what their encounters with Jesus had in common.

There was a man from the Pharisees named Nicodemus, a ruler of the Jews. This man came to Him at night and said, "Rabbi, we know that You have come from God as a teacher, for no one could perform these signs You do unless God were with him."

Jesus replied, "I assure you: Unless someone is born again, he cannot see the kingdom of God."

"But how can anyone be born when he is old?" Nicodemus asked Him. "Can he enter his mother's womb a second time and be born?"

Jesus answered, "I assure you: Unless someone is born of water and the Spirit, he cannot enter the kingdom of God.

JOHN 3:1-5

Jesus began His conversation with a spiritual truth that intrigued Nicodemus (let's call him Nic) just as He did with the Samaritan woman. Both Nic and the Samaritan woman engaged in a back and forth conversation with Jesus that drew them closer to the truth. Both needed a spiritual solution to what they had been seeking in earthly things.

Of course, even people who aren't familiar with the Bible probably recognize Jesus' words to Nic later in their conversation. We'll look more closely at these words next week, since they are the gospel in a nutshell.

For God loved the world in this way: He gave His One and Only Son, so that everyone who believes in Him will not perish but have eternal life.

JOHN 3:16

The conversation in John 3:1-21 implies that Nic may have walked away not knowing exactly how he felt or what he believed about what Jesus said. You can imagine what it'd be like to replay this unexpected conversation over and over and over in your mind.

I think the writer of John's Gospel is intentionally showing us that Jesus didn't approach everyone the same way. Fishing for men (and women) is not only a matter of knowing the truth but knowing the person.

There is NO ONE-SIZE-FITS-ALL approach to evangelism.

PERSONAL STUDY 3

DON'T GIVE UP WHEN SOMEONE TRIES TO BREAK THE LINE

When it comes to matters of evangelism, Christians will often start a conversation with an area of disagreement instead of starting with what can be agree on. That is why we must listen carefully and pray for wisdom. Jesus calls us to go "fishing for men," and every fish is different.

Keeping attention on disagreements is not only a common tendency of Christians, it's often the response of the people we are fishing for. Why?

DEBATING is easier than DECIDING.

It's easier for everyone. Christians are often scared or don't know how to be intentional in how we engage other people. Many of us simply don't want to venture out into new waters. We're perfectly comfortable where we are, so why rock anybody's boat? And most non-Christians would quickly agree. If anybody ever talks about the gospel, the most comfortable way to do so is a surface conversation about religion.

It's easier for people to avoid making personal decisions about the truth if they can turn the conversation into an argument, even a friendly-natured debate. Disagreements keep things focused on impersonal facts or abstract ideas instead of heart issues and everyone's need for salvation through faith in Jesus.

I like to call this "breaking the line." When you're fishing for men and women and they try to sidetrack a conversation, it's just like a fish who has taken a bite of what you've offered but then tries to shake it off and free themselves from anything more. They realize that if they don't wiggle out of the conversation, they'll be on the hook, so to speak, for making a decision about Jesus.

Let's look again to see an example of this with the woman at the well.

Our fathers worshiped on this mountain, yet you Jews say that the place to worship is in Jerusalem.
JOHN 4:20

She tried to engage Jesus in an issue dividing people over where to worship. This happens all the time today. People aren't asking about which mountain is more holy, but they often distract the focus from the gospel to matters of musical style, personality, denomination, or politics. They are sidetracked by issues like hypocrisy, other religions, and even questions about how our reality and someone's idea of God don't seem to fit together.

Look at how Jesus responds to her attempt to break the line.

Jesus told her, "Believe Me, woman, an hour is coming when you will worship the Father neither on this mountain nor in Jerusalem. ... God is spirit, and those who worship Him must worship in spirit and truth."
JOHN 4:21,24

He acknowledges the point but keeps the focus on God and on the individual. So we can't ignore the question, even if we have to acknowledge that we don't have a great answer in the moment. We continue to stay focused on our mission of fishing for men and women. Listen. Respond. Don't overbear. But don't be intimidated. You are inviting them to know the Way, Truth, and Life.

Jesus-style evangelism is a DIALOGUE, not a MONOLOGUE.

When have you chased a rabbit or backed away from a conversation after someone had an objection, question, or point that distracted attention away from the gospel?

Tell Someone

The apostle Paul encouraged believers not to give up or be intimidated by tough questions or even direct opposition.

I am not ashamed of the gospel, because it is God's power for salvation to everyone who believes.
ROMANS 1:16

Another great example of Jesus modeling a conversation that focuses on an individual is found in the story of the rich young ruler. This man actually approaches Jesus and engages in a back-and-forth discussion that ends with a personal choice to believe or not to believe.

As He was setting out on a journey, a man ran up, knelt down before Him, and asked Him, "Good Teacher, what must I do to inherit eternal life?"

"Why do you call Me good?" Jesus asked him. "No one is good but One—God. You know the commandments:

Do not murder;
do not commit adultery;
do not steal;
do not bear false witness;
do not defraud;
honor your father and mother."

He said to Him, "Teacher, I have kept all these from my youth."

Then, looking at him, Jesus loved him and said to him, "You lack one thing: Go, sell all you have and give to the poor, and you will have treasure in heaven. Then come, follow Me." But he was stunned at this demand, and he went away grieving, because he had many possessions.
MARK 10:17-22

Jesus responds to the man's question with His own question about the man's motive in asking Jesus for an answer. Jesus then listens to the man before building on his response to turn the conversation away from a path of rules and patting oneself on the back toward a complete faith in and devotion to following Jesus.

Let's bring this back into your world today. Put yourself into Jesus' shoes—or sandals—and imagine how you might respond to questions and points today.

In the left column, write objections or arguments you've heard people use to distract from a personal decision regarding the gospel. In the right column, write a short point about how you could respond to the question in order to keep the focus on the gospel.

Breaking the Line	Focusing on the Gospel

WHAT IS THE GOSPEL?

START

Start by welcoming everyone back to the fifth session of *Tell Someone.* Ask group members the following questions to review the past week's study and to introduce this week's topic.

Last week you looked at how to share the gospel. What was helpful or encouraging as you thought through conversations about the gospel?

When have you had a recent conversation and someone broke the line or tried to break the line? How were you able to bring the focus back to the gospel?

Did anyone have an opportunity to share their testimony or have conversations about Jesus this past week? If so, what happened?

We've looked at why, when, where, and how to share the gospel. Today we'll be sure that we know exactly what the gospel is.

Pray for your time together now and then show the video for session 5.

WATCH

Use the space below to take notes as you watch session 5.

Did you miss the group session?
Video sessions are available for purchase at *lifeway.com/tellsomeone*

RESPOND

Respond to the video teaching by discussing the questions below.

READ ROMANS 1:16.

Have you ever been "ashamed of the gospel?" If so, why?

Only 1/3 of Americans know what "gospel" means. Do you feel comfortable explaining what it means? Why or why not?

Are you most likely to focus on the bad news or good news when talking to nonbelievers? Why are you prone to focus on the bad or the good? Why is it essential to communicate both the bad and good news?

READ ROMANS 3:23 AND 6:23.

What key points of the gospel are clear in these two verses?

Two definitions of sin were presented in the video: trespass (crossing a line) and missing the mark. How are these helpful definitions? How would you explain sin?

What did Greg mean when he agreed that all roads lead to God, but only one road leads to heaven?

READ REVELATION 20:11-15 AND 21:1-5

What do these verses reveal about heaven and hell? If we believe heaven and hell are real, how does that effect the gospel's urgency?

What else has been challenging or encouraging from today's session?

This week you'll think through how to explain the whole gospel. Next week we'll practice verbalizing the gospel with one another and share any opportunities you have this week to tell someone why the gospel is such good news.

PERSONAL STUDY 1

WHAT DO I SAY WHEN SHARING THE GOSPEL?

This may be the most important part of this study. If we get this wrong, most of what you have studied and discussed will not be of much help. This is the bottom line. This is the message we are called to bring to people. It's the gospel.

Based on what you know or what you've learned in this Bible study, maybe for the first time, let's look at how you would explain the basics of the gospel.

For the gospel to be GOOD NEWS we have to be aware that there is BAD NEWS.

In your own words, what is the bad news?

Why is this critical for someone to understand the bad news?

Many times we want to avoid the bad news in our politically correct and supposedly tolerant society. The very idea of getting someone to admit they have sin that needs forgiveness is not a message so well received. Essentially our society's mantra is that nobody has the right to tell others that they are "wrong" about their way of life or wrong about their understanding of God. And we definitely don't have the right to tell others that there's only one way to live eternally in heaven.

I am the way, the truth, and the life. No one comes to the Father except through Me.
JOHN 14:6

Jesus told His disciples plainly and simply the truth about life in relationship with God and that He was the only way to heaven.

This isn't narrow-minded or hateful, as some people would try to make it. This is the truth. It's reality. And it's an invitation to know the Way, Truth, and Life now and forever!

How would you explain to someone that the only way to heaven is through a relationship with Jesus?

How would you explain that this is a loving invitation rather than a hateful exclusion of people who do not believe in Jesus?

Once we get into the bad news, it's easy to move on to the good news. You might start with the benefits and blessings of God making Himself known, wanting a relationship with us, and His gift of eternal life with Him in heaven. Everyone likes the promise of eternal life, right?

There have been countless stories throughout history driven by the idea of man's natural desire for eternal life and power over death.

But don't miss this. You can't stop with the good news. You have to include the bad news and need for repentance. Otherwise you're only offering an inspirational message, a morality based self-help strategy, and ultimately false hope for life in heaven.

That's why Jesus said to repent and believe. People need to turn from their sin to put their faith in Jesus instead of in themselves and their own abilities. There's nothing anyone can do to save himself or herself.

Tell Someone

Without the bad news, people don't even realize they need a Savior. What does "being saved" even mean to someone unfamiliar with our Christian jargon? If they don't believe in hell or sin that deserves an eternal existence separated from God instead of with Him, from what do they need saving?

Hell isn't popular to talk about. It sure isn't popular to believe that seemingly good people are in danger of spending eternity in a real place of suffering and judgment for sin. But it *is* real. And people desperately need saving whether they know it or not!

Only Jesus can save them, but He has chosen to work through believers to awaken people to this reality and to the good news of salvation through faith in Jesus.

Circle key words identifying gospel truths in each of the following verses.

"I [Jesus] have come so that they may have life and have it in abundance."
JOHN 10:10

All have sinned and fall short of the glory of God.
ROMANS 3:23

The wages of sin is death, but the gift of God is eternal life in Christ Jesus our Lord.
ROMANS 6:23

God proves His own love for us in that while we were still sinners, Christ died for us!
ROMANS 5:8

For I passed on to you as most important what I also received:
Christ died for our sins
according to the Scriptures,
that He was buried,
that He was raised on the third day
according to the Scriptures.
1 CORINTHIANS 15:3-4

"I am the way, the truth, and the life. No one comes to the Father except through Me."
JOHN 14:6

"God loved the world in this way: He gave His One and Only Son, so that everyone who believes in Him will not perish but have eternal life."
JOHN 3:16

If you only had one verse to share the gospel, John 3:16 is one of the most recognizable verses in the whole Bible. It's a concise summary of the good news and bad news.

In your own words, write a concise gospel presentation.

PERSONAL STUDY 2

THERE'S BAD NEWS & THERE'S GOOD NEWS

We've all heard those "good news/bad news" jokes. But there really is bad news—we've all broken God's commandments and we fall short of His standards. Even if you have a clear gospel presentation and plan for a conversation, that doesn't mean the other person will automatically respond. We've prepared for this reality in previous weeks. When we maintain a personal focus, the person is presented with both the bad news and the good news of the gospel.

When I share with people that the Bible says, "All have sinned and fall short of the glory of God" (Rom. 3:23), there are three common responses:

AWARENESS

Some people are aware of the "bad news" even if they don't know exactly what it is. People who respond in this way are aware of their brokenness, admit their problems, and feel burdened by an inability to fix things on their own. They have tried different things to bring peace, pleasure, or purpose to their lives. Even if their efforts seemed to work for a while, they're ultimately left feeling empty and still searching for "something" that they can't identify.

These people may be caught in an addiction or pattern of behavior they want to break. Or they may feel worthless due to things they've done or that have been done to them. They may not have a background or understanding that would allow them to categorize the problems as sin, but they know there's something wrong and they want to believe there is "good news."

Imagine speaking to someone who is aware of the "bad news" but doesn't recognize it as sin. What would you say?

ANGER

Another common response is anger. This type of response may seem like a worst-case scenario, but it really isn't. While it may be the most intimidating response, anger usually reveals an awareness of sin.

What looks like anger can be a reaction to pain. Imagine that you fell and broke your leg. But when I go to help you, you get loud, pull away, or push me away. Even though you know you have a problem, your natural reaction is to just stop the pain in that moment. On top of the pain, you might be ashamed about how you got hurt or hate the idea of looking weak and needing help.

When addressing the reality of sin, what comes out as anger is really pain or pride. A person is fully aware of the problem, but it hurts and it's humbling. So while this may be your greatest fear in evangelism, especially in sharing the gospel with someone you love, it's really a sign that the person is hurting.

We've all heard people defensively say that you shouldn't "judge" them. Look at what Jesus said about the good news of the gospel and judgment.

> *God loved the world in this way: He gave His One and Only Son, so that everyone who believes in Him will not perish but have eternal life. For God did not send His Son into the world that He might condemn the world, but that the world might be saved through Him. Anyone who believes in Him is not condemned, but anyone who does not believe is already condemned, because he has not believed in the name of the One and Only Son of God.*
> **JOHN 3:16-18**

How is sharing the gospel a loving thing to do rather than hurtful or judgmental?

How can your story help show that "all have sinned" (Rom. 3:23), even you?

ACCEPTANCE

Finally, another response to sin is to say, "I try to be a good person." Sometimes these are the hardest conversations to have—people don't see any need for salvation when they don't feel the bad news applies to their lives. They're generally nice, hardworking, and generous people. Life is pretty good in their opinion.

Many people believe their lives are acceptable according to some moral standard. Their standard doesn't come from a biblical understanding of God and sin. They may protest and say things like, "I'm not a sinner," believing that sin is only the big, bad things that everyone would view as wrong.

If a person acknowledges any wrong, they respond with, "nobody's perfect." But the Bible is clear that "all have sinned and fall short" of God's standard, which is perfection. God is holy and perfect. To be in relationship with Him, we have to be perfect, too. We can't simply compare ourselves to one another to see if we're just as good or better than the average person. None of us pass the test when it comes to God's standard.

God doesn't grade on a CURVE.
He grades on the CROSS.

How would you explain sin to someone?

Two phrases that help to explain sin are "missing the mark" and "crossing the line," which is how the biblical word *trespass* translates. The Bible says we are "dead in [our] trespasses and sins" (Eph. 2:1). When we break the Commandments it's like we are crossing the "No trespassing" line.

This is where the Ten Commandments can help the person you are speaking with understand what sin is. The Bible doesn't give us a list of rules to keep in order to earn our way into heaven. The Bible says that nobody can perfectly keep the commands—and that's the point!

Obviously, the law applies to those to whom it was given, for its purpose is to keep people from having excuses, and to show that the entire world is guilty before God.
ROMANS 3:19, NLT

So, when explaining the bad news of sin, simply asking whether or not a person has broken any of the Ten Commandments is an easy place to start. Ask them:

□ **Have you ever stolen anything?**

□ **Have you ever told a lie?"**

□ **Have you ever wanted something that wasn't yours?**

□ **Have you ever disrespected your parents?**

The answer to at least one of these questions is obviously yes! Most people will admit to breaking these commands. But those are just little sins right? The Bible says all sin, no matter how big or small we think it may be, separates us from God. We're guilty. Once we've sinned, we're sinners needing a Savior.

Whoever keeps the entire law, yet fails in one point, is guilty of breaking it all.
JAMES 2:10

People will respond, "But I'm still a good person!" You might say something like: "I'm sure you are in many ways a good person, but you can't be good enough or do enough good things to get into heaven."

Heaven isn't for GOOD people;
it's for FORGIVEN people.

And that brings us to the bottom line of the gospel. The only person who has ever kept all of the Commandments perfectly was Jesus Christ. That is why He, and He alone, is uniquely qualified to bridge the gap between sinful humanity and a holy God whom we all repeatedly offend through our sin. It's the death of Jesus Christ on the cross for all sinners and His resurrection from the dead that gets us into heaven.

I love the way Paul personalized it in Galatians 2:20 when he said that the Son of God "loved me and gave Himself for me." What was true of Paul is true of me, you, and the people all around you. The bad news of sin applies to every one of us. That's why every one of us needs to hear the good news about Jesus!

PERSONAL STUDY 3

SHARING GOD'S WORD IN A LANGUAGE PEOPLE UNDERSTAND

We need to have a good working knowledge of how to share the essential gospel message. In previous sessions, we've discussed the essential elements. But when it comes to sharing the gospel, it seems we tend to lean to one of two extremes: either to add to or take away from.

We've studied how the gospel is made up of both bad and good news. To understand and believe in the good news, a person must understand and admit his or her part in the bad news. It's easy to soften the message in a desire not to offend or have an uncomfortable conversation. We may want to skip over the seriousness of sin or the commitment to Jesus as the only way to be right with God and live forever in heaven. But taking away from the message means we're left with something less than the full truth. It's not the gospel at all.

Scripture is clear about what God requires for salvation. Too often we add elements that are not essential to the core message, like baptism or good works as essential requirements for salvation. Those are good things but should come after a person believes. To miss this is to get the cart before the horse.

In what ways are you prone to add to or take away from the gospel?

Don't add this to the gospel

Don't take this away from the gospel

The two most important things in sharing the gospel are WHAT we say and HOW we say it.

Besides changing the message, one of the biggest problems for Christians when it comes to telling people what Jesus has done for them, is our vocabulary. We probably don't even realize we're speaking a language they don't understand!

If you've grown up in a Christian family or been in a church very long, you're used to words that are likely unfamiliar to someone whose background doesn't include the church. Our religious terms, biblical phrases, and seemingly archaic language don't make sense to a nonbeliever.

If you've ever spoken to a friend who has a hobby or career with a specialized language, you know what this feels like. Take for example a conversation about computers. You may have a basic awareness of computers, but when the conversation starts including terms like RAM and ROM or inside jokes about users of different operating systems, you feel awkward and lost. The language not only doesn't make sense, it can alienate you and make you feel like an outsider. The person you are talking to may not even realize that what is normal for him or her is completely foreign to you and the average person.

This happens with Christians. The religious insider language is often called "Christianese." It might as well be a foreign language.

As Christians we may be out of touch with the people we are speaking to. Perhaps this is due in part to submerging ourselves in a Christian subculture. For instance, imagine what nonbelievers might think when they hear things like "being washed in the blood." They might think you're crazy! As believers, we understand that you are speaking of being cleansed of sin and being made right with God through Jesus' sacrifice on the cross.

Biblical imagery like sacrifice and theological vocabulary like justified and sanctified may not mean much if anything to someone unfamiliar with the Bible or the church.

Tell Someone

The gospel can get LOST IN TRANSLATION
if you're speaking "CHRISTIANESE."

Use the space below to write down some biblical phrases a nonbeliever may not understand and then write out a way you could explain that same idea in everyday language.

Christianese	Everyday Language

Look back at your summary of the gospel on page 83 to see if you've used any "Christianese" that needs to be clarified for a nonbeliever.

To be clear, I'm not suggesting you not use biblical terminology when sharing your faith. I am simply saying you can't expect that the average nonbeliever would know what you are talking about. But I do believe we want to quote and use Scripture in our evangelism.

You can carry a Bible or access it on an electronic device, but the best place to hide God's Word is in your heart. When you quote Scripture, you don't have to shout it or quote it in an "other-worldly" way. You can, in a conversational manner, share the Word of God.

The days are gone when most people had a basic understanding of the gospel. In fact, research shows that the fastest growing religious group in America is the "Nones." When people are asked to identify their religious belief, they check the box labeled "none." Most people simply don't have a religious background or strong spiritual beliefs anymore.

Most people today aren't like the people gathered on the day of Pentecost, when Peter preached and 3,000 believed. Those people were biblically literate and understood certain scriptural ideas. Our audience today would be more like the crowd assembled at Mars Hill in Athens, to whom Paul spoke in Acts 17. They were biblically illiterate, more familiar with Greek philosophers and poets. They were a completely secular culture.

So, how do we reach a culture that thinks like this? We reach our culture the same way the first-century believers reached their culture: with the powerful message of the gospel. This is why Paul said:

"I am not ashamed of the gospel, because it is
God's power for salvation to everyone who believes,
first to the Jew, and also to the Greek."
ROMANS 1:16

The Greek word Paul uses that translates to "power" is *dunamis*. It's the root word for dynamite. Paul is telling us that there is explosive power in the essential gospel message. Paul assessed the situation and adapted accordingly. We must do the same today, starting with speaking in a language that people understand.

Write a prayer for confidence in the power of the gospel and an awareness of how to share it in a way that people can understand.

WEEK 6

CLOSE THE DEAL

START

Start by welcoming everyone back to the final session of *Tell Someone*. Ask group members the following questions to review the past week's study and to introduce this week's topic.

Last week you answered the question: *What is the gospel?* **What was most helpful as you identified the basic gospel message?**

Can everyone share a one-minute version of the gospel in your own words? (Encourage each person to do this, even if it sounds redundant, so that everyone can practice speaking the gospel message to other people.)

Did anyone have an opportunity to share the gospel this past week? If so, what happened?

Over the past six weeks we've looked at what the gospel is and why, when, where, and how to share the gospel. Today we'll wrap it all up as Greg and his wife, Cathe, discuss what to do *after* sharing the gospel.

Pray for your time together as a group and then show the video for session 6.

WATCH

Use the space below to take notes as you watch session 6.

Did you miss the group session?
Video sessions are available for purchase at *lifeway.com/tellsomeone*

RESPOND

Respond to the video teaching by discussing the questions below.

How would you describe the way you felt about evangelism before this study, compared to the way you feel now?

How have you been challenged or encouraged during this series? What has been most helpful?

What is your biggest fear in sharing the gospel? If willing to share the gospel, why are we often afraid to ask for a decision?

READ MATTHEW 28:18-20.

Has your understanding of the Great Commission changed during this series? If so, how?

Evangelism isn't as complicated as we make it, and neither is discipleship. Discipleship isn't just a class; it's learning through life together.

What person has been the greatest example to you of a Christian life?

What in your life would change if you kept in mind the fact that people are looking to you as an example?

Have you brought someone to church? What was your experience?

How can you be helpful to your church instead of critical?

Remember, you may not be a Paul, but we can all be a Barnabas who comes alongside someone to encourage a new Christian.

In the final pages of this book you'll find exercises to help you think through the steps after sharing the gospel, followed by a personal plan of action.

PERSONAL STUDY 1

YOU HAVE TO ASK FOR A RESPONSE

It's been said that it's important to:

Keep the MAIN THING the main thing.

That sounds obvious and even pointless, but so often we do get sidetracked on secondary issues, at best. In our study we've identified ways people attempt to break the line when we try to bring them to Christ.

The whole point of evangelism isn't to be nice, it's not to prove your point, it's not even to mention the Bible or invite someone to church (although those things are great, as we'll see this week). The "main thing" in evangelism is to verbally articulate the gospel and to ask for a personal response. We don't even want to simply speak the truth. Why would we share the truth of abundant and eternal life without asking for a person to respond to that reality?

Now is the time we start wrapping things up, gathering together the various pieces from the last five weeks. Each simple step you've taken has brought you to the most important moment.

This is what sharing the gospel is all about. This is key to completing the mission Jesus assigned to every one who follows Him by faith.

It's not enough to TELL someone.
You also have to ASK someone.

You have to pop the big question. You have to close the deal. You have to bring in the net as you fish for men and women in the name of Jesus.

You know what it is. If we stop at explaining the truth about Jesus, we leave our mission of going to make disciples incomplete.

Just like there's no one-size fits all conversation or presentation of the gospel, there's no one way to ask for a response. Just ask for a response.

"Would you like to put your faith in Jesus right now?"
"Why not ask His forgiveness right now?"
"Why not accept His free gift of grace and the promise of eternal life with Him in heaven?"

What excuses have you made for not asking people to make a decision?

What is your fear or concern with asking people to make a decision?

Check and add any ways you've asked someone to do something other than make a personal decision for faith in Jesus.

□ **Visit your church**

□ **Come to your small group**

□ **Hang out with some of your Christian friend**

□ **Attend a Christian event**

□ **Read a Christian book**

□ **Listen to Christian music**

□ **Other**

Obviously these are all great things and we should encourage each of those things (depending on what you may have written in the "other" space).

Tell Someone

But Jesus was very specific in the Great Commission. He said to make disciples, teaching them to live out everything He commanded and baptize them. These are essential parts of the community of God people.

Remember in the Great Commission Jesus didn't just give us this amazing assignment of eternal significance, He promised to be with us as we go.

His Spirit equips, empowers, and enables our ability to share the gospel as well as other people's responses to this good news.

So let's look back at the steps that have brought you to this point and then to see where to go from here.

Write down ways that feel comfortable and natural for you to ask people to make a decision.

If someone is ready to make a decision of faith, the first step is leading them in what is sometimes called the "sinner's prayer." There is not a specific prayer in Scripture that we can lead them in so I suggest something along the lines of the following. This prayer emphasizes a personal response to the key message of the gospel. I will usually ask them to pray it out loud after me.

Lord Jesus,
I know that I am a sinner.
But I also know that You are Savior.
Forgive me of my sins.
I repent of them now, and I choose to follow You from this moment forward as my Savior and Lord, my God and Friend.
Thank You for dying on the cross for me and rising again from the dead.
I ask You to come into my life.
I choose to follow You from this day forward.
Thank You for loving me and calling me and accepting me.
In Jesus' name I pray.
Amen.

You're on your way to an exciting adventure, experiencing God at work in and through you in ways you never dreamed possible. Get ready to join Him in the fulfilling this great mission.

"All authority has been given to Me in heaven and on earth. Go, therefore, and make disciples of all nations, baptizing them in the name of the Father and of the Son and of the Holy Spirit, teaching them to observe everything I have commanded you. And remember, I am with you always, to the end of the age."
MATTHEW 28:18–20

"Go into all the world and preach the gospel to the whole creation."
MARK 16:15, NLT

At the end of this book you have a place to gather some practical steps that you've identified over the past six weeks. It can serve as a map of sorts as you seek to "go into all the world."

So now that you know how to share the good news ...

TELL SOMEONE!

PERSONAL STUDY 2

ALWAYS BE READY TO BE USED BY GOD

Always be ready to give a defense to everyone who asks you a reason for the hope that is in you.
1 PETER 3:15

The word for "defense" in the Greek is *apologia* which means "a defense or justification of a belief." We have to be ready to explain the bad news of guilt and sin along with the good news of grace and forgiveness in Jesus.

Every Christian who wants to lead others to Christ needs to have at least a basic understanding of his or her faith and how to answer difficult and oft-asked questions. We need, to the best of our ability, to try to answer the difficult questions people ask and then pivot back to our main objective: Jesus Christ and Him crucified.

We have to share the gospel and ask for a response. This is where it falls apart for most Christians: closing the deal or pulling in the net. How do we make that transition from sharing our testimony and the essential gospel message to actually leading another person to Christ? It's not as hard as you may think. But you have to ask the question sooner or later: "Would you like to ask Jesus Christ into your heart right now?"

I never pressure a person to believe and neither should you. As much as we may want someone to believe, we can't force or manufacture a genuine decision. Nobody can make someone else believe. But we can tell someone the good news and ask him or her to believe.

Our job is PROCLAMATION, not MANIPULATION.

What's the difference between proclamation and manipulation?

What's the difference between pressure and persistence?

Remember, it's not a matter of your ability. It's a matter of your availability. Your job is not to be able to argue someone into saying they believe in Jesus. Your job is to be available for God to work through you. This doesn't mean you shouldn't be ready—this whole study has been equipping you to be ready to share the gospel.

This reminds me of the biblical story of a man of great importance who came to the city of Jerusalem looking for truth. (See Acts 8:26-40.) Instead of the vibrant faith of the former glory days of Jewish history, he found a dead, lifeless orthodoxy. But this foreign dignitary, no doubt because of his importance, did leave the city with something of great value: a personal copy of the scroll of Isaiah the prophet.

Scripture tells us this man was the treasurer for the Queen of Ethiopia, so he probably traveled in a caravan with a large entourage. As he left Jerusalem, he was riding in his chariot, reading out loud from Isaiah 53, trying to make some rhyme or reason out of it. Isaiah 53 prophetically speaks of the suffering of the Messiah hundreds of years before it happened. And God had the right man in the right place at the right time to intercept him and answer this spiritually hungry man's questions. Talk about divine appointments.

The man God chose was a follower of Jesus named Philip, and he'd just been directed by the Lord to go to the desert and wait. (See Acts 8:26.) No detailed blueprint. No battle plan. God directed him to just go to the desert and wait. That is how God usually leads us: one step at a time.

Philip may have been frustrated, standing in the blazing sun and wondering how this was a good idea—until he saw this large caravan approaching with this foreign dignitary, identified as the Ethiopian Eunuch, reading aloud from Isaiah's book. Philip does something that is very important when it comes to sharing our faith: he said the right thing at the right time.

Philip used something that is missing in many evangelistic endeavors: tact.

Tact is saying the RIGHT THING at the RIGHT TIME in the RIGHT WAY.

Tell Someone

Other words for tact are diplomacy, sensitivity, savoir faire. Tact is simply skill and grace in dealing with others. Isaac Newton said:

> Tact is the art of making a POINT
> without making an ENEMY.

When sharing the gospel, how can you lack tact by saying the right thing in the wrong way? Write some examples of tactless evangelism.

Philip tactfully asks the man from Ethiopia, "Do you understand what you're reading?" (v. 30). Philip didn't push himself on this man; he asked him a simple and straightforward question. Much to his delight, the dignitary responds, "How can I … unless someone guides me?" And then he "invited Philip to come up and sit with him" (v. 31).

Philip explained the Scriptures to this searching man, and it resulted in his conversion that day. He was even baptized on the spot! The man needed someone to instruct him—to show him the way. I love the way the story ends. We read that the man from Ethiopia "went on his way rejoicing" (Acts 8:39).

Describe a time when you may have missed an opportunity to share the gospel. What caused you to miss that opportunity?

What will you tell yourself in order to seize the moment and share the gospel?

How can you stay prepared?

Now to wrap up this idea of readiness, think back to the apostle Paul and his words that started this portion of your personal study. Paul was not only a great evangelist, boldly proclaiming the gospel, he was also a great disciple-maker. We'll talk more about him in Personal Study 3, but look at what he says to Timothy, a young man into whom he was pouring godly wisdom regarding the Christian life. The verse below comes from a letter Paul wrote to Timothy.

Proclaim the message; persist in it whether convenient or not.
2 TIMOTHY 4:2

Another translation says:

Preach the word; be ready in season and out of season.
2 TIMOTHY 4:2, ESV

Summarize Paul's encouragement in 2 Timothy 4:2 and how it relates to sharing the gospel in your own life.

You've studied what to say and how to say it. Be ready. You never know when an opportunity may present itself to change somebody's life forever!

PERSONAL STUDY 3

LEADING PEOPLE TOWARD THEIR NEXT STEPS

So, let's say God has graciously allowed you to lead a person to Christ. Is that the end? Actually, it's just the beginning! Now it is your privilege to disciple him or her. But what does that mean? Let's go back to the Great Commission.

> *"Go, therefore, and make disciples of all nations, baptizing them in the name of the Father and of the Son and of the Holy Spirit, teaching them to observe everything I have commanded you. And remember, I am with you always, to the end of the age."*
> **MATTHEW 28:19-20**

Note that phrase, "teaching them to observe everything I have commanded you." Your job is to take this person under your wing and help him or her to acclimate to a new commitment to follow Christ. You don't need to be a Bible scholar to do this. In fact, in many ways you just need to be a friend. You need to model what a follower of Jesus Christ looks like in the real world. You want to help this person grow up spiritually.

It could be compared to having a newborn baby or small child around. Children are fickle. They can go from laughing to crying in a millisecond (sometimes doing both at once). They can go from total happiness to complete misery. Young believers can be very vulnerable as well. They need older believers to stabilize them and ground them in their faith.

Jesus didn't say to go make CONVERTS.
Jesus said to go make DISCIPLES.

Repenting from sin and believing in Jesus is the first step of faith. To believers Jesus says, "Come, follow me, and I will show you how to fish for people!"

(Matt. 4:19, NLT). He's made you a fisher of men and you've drawn in the net. But where do we go from here? Following Jesus isn't just a single step. Now we want to help people take the next steps.

A poll by researcher George Barna revealed that about 25 percent of the adults in the United States would go to church if a friend invited them. Barna elaborated, "The best chance of getting them to a church is when someone they know and trust invites them and offers to accompany them."

That is an amazing statistic. Think about it for a moment: 25 percent of the people out there are waiting for an invitation to go to church.

The key is to invite them. And more to the point, you pick them up and take them with you. If the pastor doesn't extend an invitation for people to come to Christ in the service, you could go out for lunch afterward and have that conversation with them. If they make a decision of faith or have already come to faith, their next step is to join a community of believers where they can grow.

Most people come to church because someone invites them. Most people come to faith because someone shares the gospel with them.

Write down the names of people you can invite to church.

To be sure you're ready to help people take this important step of getting involved in a local church, fill out the following information.

Name of Church:

Address:

Time of Worship:

Website:

If the person is a new believer, invite him or her into relationship with other Christians through a small group or Bible study. Your church may also offer a class for new believers or new members. You'll want to be sure any new Christian has a Bible, ideally one with study notes to explain what he or she is reading. Recommend the translation that your church uses most often for preaching or teaching. Don't overwhelm someone but be ready to offer help.

Write down any recommendations that could be helpful to a new Christian.

Bible study groups or classes:

Recommended Bibles and Bible apps:

Favorite Christian books, sermons, podcasts:

Make yourself available to meet with, talk to, and encourage a new believer. This can be a natural rhythm or a more established time to be intentional about studying and discussing God's Word. If you've begun a relationship with a new Christian, write down a time and place you can meet to disciple him or her one-on-one.

I can't emphasize enough how important it is to integrate these new believers into your local church. Jesus only started one organization when He walked this earth, and that was the church. Jesus loves the church, and so should we. We can't grow spiritually without being an active member and participant in a local church.

The church is like an oasis of HOPE in
a desert of HOPELESSNESS.

In the epistle to the Ephesians, Paul talks about how God "personally gave some to be apostles, some prophets, some evangelists, some pastors and teachers, for the training of the saints in the work of ministry, to build up the body of Christ" (Eph. 4:11-12). Every new believer needs a pastor. For that matter, every mature believer needs a pastor, too.

The apostle Paul wasn't always the great preacher and author of New Testament epistles. He was known as Saul, an infamous "Christian-killer." I can guarantee that Saul never intended to convert to the Christian faith, much less become one of its greatest leaders. When Saul was stopped and blinded while traveling to Damascus to persecute Christians, he had no idea what was happening. Then he heard those powerful and ominous words, "Saul, Saul, why are you persecuting Me?" (Acts 9:4).

The key word in that question is "Me." The voice continued, "I am Jesus, the One you are persecuting!" (Acts 9:5). Jesus values and identifies with the church so much that to persecute the church is to persecute Christ Himself.

Saul believed on the spot, but who would ever believe this man's life had been changed by Jesus? Answer: pretty much no one. But the Lord also spoke to a man named Ananias about Saul. God told him to go seek out this unlikely convert. (See Acts 9:11.) This would be like a Jew who was hiding from the Nazis hearing that Adolf Hitler had been saved and was seeking him out!

To Ananias' eternal credit, he obeyed the Lord, sought out Saul, prayed for him, and assured him. What would have happened to Saul without Ananias? Saul needed a friend, just like every new believer does.

Ananias was truly an unsung hero of the Christian faith. He never preached any sermons that we know of. He never performed miracles. He never wrote an epistle. But he did reach one who did all of that and more.

If we had more Ananiases, we would have more Pauls. You may not be the next Billy Graham, but you may be the person who nurtures and encourages the next Billy Graham. Like Ananias, and maybe even like Paul, Jesus is calling you to preach the gospel and make disciples.

USE THE FOLLOWING PAGES TO PUT TOGETHER AN ACTION PLAN OR HOW YOU CAN TELL SOMEONE THE GOOD NEWS.

YOUR PERSONAL PLAN
TO TELL SOMEONE THE GOOD NEWS

Week 1

With whom can you share the gospel?

Week 2

When and where can you share the gospel?

Week 3

What's your testimony?

Tell Someone

Week 4

How can you respond to objections?

Week 5

What's the gospel?

Week 6
How will you ask for a decision?

What will you lead someone to pray?

Now go... TELL SOMEONE!